Cost-Effective Information Systems

Cost-Effective Information Systems

Burton J. Cohen

American Management Association, Inc.

This book has been distributed without charge to AMA members enrolled in the Finance, Management Systems and Sciences, General Management, and General Services Divisions.

International standard book number: 0–8144–2152–0
Library of Congress catalog card number: 78–152375

To Jane
and
Paul, Josh, and Dougie

Foreword

THE role of the information systems function in many industries underwent a major transition during the 1960s. In the future, that role will continue to change, as will the role of economists, planning specialists, and others in support functions. The extent of that change will depend on the degree to which those functions can perceive the business objectives which they support, and the degree to which those perceptions can be translated into action that contributes to attaining or exceeding those objectives, or possibly even to refining or improving them.

This book is not a technical presentation, but rather a set of guidelines which, if tailored to the individual requirements of a specific firm, should help the information systems function to relate to the needs of the enterprise it serves in a businesslike, cost-effective way.

I would like to thank James E. Seitz, Touche Ross & Co., National Director of Management Services Operations, and Harvey D. Braun, a Principal in the Management Services Division of Touche Ross & Co., for taking time out of their busy schedules to review this book, which resulted in a number of improvements to its content.

Burton J. Cohen

Contents

1   **Foundation of the Cost-Effectiveness Program**   11

   Strategic Versus Tactical Planning
   Criteria for Successful Systems
   Control Points

2   **Cost-Effective Environmental Management**   20

   Upper Management Involvement
   Information Systems Council
   Identification of Requirements
   Priority Setting
   Cost Justification
   User Charging as a Management Tool
   Review of Existing Systems
   Confirming Major Decisions
   Consistency with Long-Range Planning
   Defining Working Relationships

3   **Cost-Effective People Management**   35

   The Interview
   Consistency
   Clear Definition of Assignments

Performance Measurement
Functional Orientation

4   **Cost-Effective Project Management**   39

Control Systems for Large Projects
Control Systems for Small Projects
Major Project Activities
Project Control
Problem Activities
Reporting on Progress

5   **Cost-Effective Production Management**   53

Measuring Actual Computer Time
Program Testing
Budget Control

6   **Organization**   59

Information Systems Within Firm
Within Information Systems
Systems Evaluation and Control

1

Foundation of the
Cost-Effectiveness Program

In many firms the information systems function has failed to live up to its potential. Although there are various reasons for this failure, two major conditions account for many of the problems that exist.

First, because of their overly technical orientation, the people in the information systems function often fail to relate technical capabilities to business needs, thus reducing the effectiveness of the information systems function. Second, the responsible executive is often not actively involved in the information systems planning and control process.

These two conditions combine to form a vicious cycle. In discussing plans and problems with his information systems staff, the executive often hears a great deal of unnecessary technical jargon which leads him to withdraw further from direct involvement with that group. Thus, he abdicates his responsibility to lead the function into becoming an effective support mechanism in the company. Because of his abdication, the information systems people do not receive the functional leadership and guidance they need, and their reaction is to retreat more into their technical shell and to become even less responsive to functional requirements.

Although the executive does not need to be involved in the details of the function, he must be directly involved in the planning, priority-setting process, and major decision making that occur in the information systems function. It is inevitable that functional areas will make a wide variety of requests for designs or modification of systems. Because some of these requests will conflict, and others will complement each other, often combining several requests into one system would be the truly effective way to design. Information systems personnel must assist in the requests for definitions and must perceive the commonality of those requests to the greatest extent possible.

However, when all the assessments have been completed and all functional areas heard from, only one person can effectively approve a priority list for systems development in the firm. That person is the executive in charge of the information systems function.

Strategic Versus Tactical Planning

Cost effectiveness can be approached from both the strategic and the tactical points of view. The most significant results, however, will be achieved only through careful attention to strategy, that is, through detailed identification of projects and concentrated attention to the priority-setting process. The best project control system in the world will not render cost effective a system that has not been well conceived and defined. The essence of the cost-effectiveness program can succeed or fail in the beginning stages, before a project is even defined.

However, from the tactical viewpoint, there are, of course, the day-to-day operating problems of existing projects which have far exceeded budget, of existing staffs which may or may not be user oriented, and of existing applications whose costs of operation are rendering the systems cost ineffective. This book will review both the strategic and the tactical approaches to cost-effective information systems.

Criteria for Successful Systems

Five basic criteria must be applied in order for a system to be successful. Although these points are fairly obvious, I have seen systems designed and implemented without consideration of one or more of them. In such cases negative ramifications inevitably ripple through the organization, and task forces are then organized to determine why these points weren't considered in the first place. Therefore, obvious as these criteria are, we should review them and keep them in mind during the planning and project-selection process.

Relevance. The first, and paramount, point is the relevance of the system to serve a stated business need. It is critical to articulate clearly the objective of the system, to specify who will use it and how they will relate to it, and to describe how the system will satisfy the stated objective.

Sometimes an area in a company tries to solve a problem by computerizing it, on the assumption that the computer itself is the cure rather than the vehicle to be used to solve an operating or planning problem. Such situations generally end up in a computerized mess rather than a manual mess. The computerized problem is more expensive and more difficult to solve than it would have been had it been approached properly in the first place.

Another example of the importance of relevance is the staff man in headquarters who says: "Now this is what the field organization really needs in order to function more effectively," and then works with the information systems people to define, design, and implement a system. When it hits the field, the field organization says: "Oh, my gosh, here's something else from headquarters that I don't need." How many systems have been designed to assist the field organization to do its job better without consulting anyone in the field? How many reports are being printed by computers across the country at this very instant that will either be piled neatly in a corner or thrown away without being read because the intended users considered them irrelevant to serve their business needs? Part of this problem can be solved by user education, which can point out how the reports should be read and applied. But in many situations the reports are really not useful at all.

Timeliness. The second major criterion for successful systems is timeliness. In a missile guidance system, response time is needed in a matter of microseconds. In an airline reservations system, a response time of one to five seconds is the design criterion. In most business systems, response time of a day to a week is considered acceptable.

It is critical to define the response criteria in advance of implementation, for if they cannot be achieved it is often better not to proceed with the system at all than to design and implement what would have been a good system within an appropriate time frame but which is not useful within the actual time frame.

Economy. The third major criterion of a successful system is economy, which is, of course, the basic determinant of cost effectiveness. However, the problem is not as simple as it appears. It would be easy if the company said: "Show me the cost and the savings, and if the savings exceed the cost we go ahead, and if not we don't." But suppose a user says: "Yes, it's true that the tangible savings are less than the stated costs, but certain intangible benefits that are difficult to quantify in dollar terms are nonetheless present, and even though the costs of a system may exceed the tangible benefits, I believe the intangible value more than makes up for the difference."

With that statement we have entered the world of the subjective, in which the economy issue is not always clear. At this point the executive in charge of the information systems function must agree that the system is in fact cost effective; if he does not believe that, he must challenge the user to further define the intangible benefits before deciding whether or not to develop the system.

Accuracy. The fourth major criterion of successful systems is accuracy. Although the inclusion of adequate controls is often taken for granted, many systems are installed without them. When this happens, users who may have been enthusiastic about the system when it was conceived begin to realize that they cannot rely on the accuracy of the reports they receive, and they begin to devise manual systems that will give them the accurate data required to operate their business. I have seen elaborate, sophisticated systems which, when required to balance batches of data on input or to compare output reports to predefined totals, revealed that they lacked basic controls, checks, or balances.

Suppose that you currently have a computerized system which is not being used and that you also have a duplicate manual system which, although recognized as inefficient by users, is nonetheless necessary in order for them to perform their function. This situation represents one of the worst kinds of cost ineffectiveness and is not uncommon. Thoughtful consideration of the requirements for system controls at the time of design can usually prevent this situation from developing.

Flexibility. Flexibility, the fifth primary characteristic of successful systems, can be subdivided into two parts. The first is flexibility to handle normal growth for a period into the future. This is a balancing problem, because you do not want your system to become obsolete when you experience a 10 percent growth; nor do you want a system which is using only 10 percent of present capacity although it could handle almost unlimited growth. What you should plan is a system that is maximizing utilization at any point in time, but can be extended in a modular way so that equipment and other necessary elements can be added as growth occurs. Such a system is efficient because it can operate at close to the capacity of a given equipment configuration, but can also be expanded with little redesign or reprogramming when normal growth occurs. Unfortunately, many companies spend too much money redesigning and reprogramming systems because they did not plan a modular design when they originally implemented the system.

The second part of this criterion is flexibility in handling the inevitable changes in the planning process or the operations of the company. The need for flexibility in this area varies, of course, with the management running the company and with the nature of the business. For example, there is less likelihood of system changes in a static management operating a static business than in a management which is constantly trying to improve the planning process in a high-technology business. In the latter situation, management should probably be prepared to make significant changes in any system it puts into operation, because a system that is not flexible enough to handle the changes can very quickly become obsolete and highly cost ineffective.

Of course it is impossible to visualize every future contingency, but if attention is given to flexibility during the stages of initial requirements definition, and general design, it will usually pay for itself many times over in future operations.

Control Points

There are four distinct areas of management control that will lead to a cost-effective information systems function. Each area is critical, and unless management gives proper attention to those areas there is little possibility of establishing a cost-effective information systems activity.

Environmental management. This does not mean air-pollution control, but rather an organizational climate which is conducive to appropriate relationships between information systems personnel and users. Among other things, this means (1) establishing both an ordered method of identifying requirements for priority setting within each area and an overall priority list of development; (2) agreeing on a focus so that problems may be resolved quickly; (3) making sure that the information systems function is aware of the long-range plans of the firm so that systems can be developed consistent with those plans; (4) establishing a user-charging concept if one is needed; and (5) assigning explicit responsibilities and procedures for project-cost justification and defining clearly the working relationships of both management and nonmanagement personnel so that the result is not only an effective *planning* mechanism but also an effective mechanism to *implement*.

People management. No information systems function can be effective without a conscientious application of sound management practices in regard to people. Management must (1) develop a well-defined recruiting program and execute it carefully, (2) practice consistency in the management of staff personnel, (3) spell out clearly specific responsibilities in project assignments, (4) establish a planned program for performance evaluation, and (5) be able to motivate staff members on the basis of the business purposes of their activities. Without a well-motivated staff, schedules will tend to slip and project management systems will show wide variances between planned and actual costs and target dates.

Project management. In theory, this control takes place after projects have been selected and priorities defined. However, it is not uncommon to embark on a project before its scope has been defined and its place on the priority list fully explored. This failure should be rectified, or it will surely result in the exercise of 20/20 hindsight at some future date.

Most problems in project control can be overcome on day one by a clear, precise, documented, and agreed-to definition of the scope of the project. Sometimes projects are begun without an explicit definition of all the intended system capabilities. That is a sure road to disaster because when the project is completed, users will inevitably say in good conscience: "I thought I would have these capabilities through this system, but I find now that I don't." Without a clear definition of a project's scope, the user finds it just about impossible to visualize all the capabilities and limitations of the system, and users who are not familiar with data processing often tend to ascribe more capabilities to a system than were intended when the project was begun. If this happens, the communications barrier begins when the project begins.

The project control system must be easy to use and easy to understand, and must be organized so that problems can be identified as early as possible. It is not enough to learn, after the fact, that a target date was not met. An early warning system must identify problems soon enough so that alternate ways of attaining the planned objectives can still be established. Problems can arise during the phases of general system design, detail system design, programming and testing, system test, or implementation. The project control system must alert all members of the project, including all involved levels of management, to the project's status, and a planned mechanism to resolve problems must complement the project control system in order for corrective action to be possible.

Production management. Once a project has been defined, designed, and implemented, it becomes a computer operations problem and is handled by the production staff of computer operators and schedulers, data preparation clerks, and input/output control clerks. It is critical that clear standards be established with respect to those elements that the operations staff expects from the systems and programming people when an application becomes operational. Those elements include run sheets, program documentation, job control, backup procedures, error recovery procedures, retention cycles of all input and output—cards, tapes, disks, printed reports, or any other type of material—and clear balancing and control procedures so that there is no doubt about the accuracy of the reports generated by the system.

Equally important, standards must be established within the computer operations area so that turnaround time between the submission of data by the user and the receipt of reports by that user can be clearly measured and evaluated. Also, clear standards of computer usage, in terms of both clock time and computer meter time, should be established so that efficiency and costs can be measured.

Staffing and equipment plans must, of course, tie in with

application development plans. Therefore, the operations budget is dependent, to some degree, on the time schedule for systems development. Although staffing plans are somewhat flexible, equipment plans generally involve lead times of two to eighteen months between ordering and delivery of equipment, depending on the specific device ordered.

This aspect is particularly critical and complex in the implementation of a real-time system. Lead times for the installation of telephone lines and data sets can often exceed that of computer hardware; therefore, it is frequently necessary to make certain equipment commitments before making a final assessment of risk on application development. Contingency plans must be established to minimize the commitments in case plans for development of an application change after the equipment has been ordered.

Another area of control in operations deals with supplies. In these days of high-speed computer printers, it is not unusual to pass $100 worth of paper through the printer in one hour. Tapes, disks, cards, and other supplies also represent a considerable expense and must be controlled through a realistic budget and other measures. Without adequate controls on production management, a system that starts out cost effective can quickly be reduced to operating with excess equipment, supplies, and staff.

2

Cost-Effective Environmental Management

A FUNCTION within a firm can be effective only if it achieves that portion of the firm's objectives for which it is responsible. Of course, the creativity within that function should generate additional objectives which, once established, become a part of the objectives of the firm itself. Therefore, the objective-setting process requires two-way communication up and down the corporate structure, resulting in a planned course of action to achieve the established objectives.

It is not likely, for example, that the manufacturing arm could be engaged in activities inconsistent with the firm's objectives. The same is true of the marketing organization where, although the focus on short-term results may work to the long-term disadvantage of the firm, the activities are nevertheless generally consistent with the firm's objectives.

Upper Management Involvement

It is as important for the activities of the information systems function to be consistent with the firm's objectives as it is for any other function. Yet in many cases the application of control by management has rendered that function not only less cost effective than it might be, but downright uneconomical.

The executive in charge of the function must be closely involved in the planning process to make sure that potential users have done enough homework on the requirements-identification process. He must see that the objectives and scope of the project are well defined, and that user requirements are documented and business objectives listed before the information systems staff begins the general systems design. He must review those objectives to assure himself that his staff will not be implementing an application that would merely be nice to have rather than one that will clearly satisfy a business need. If he does not believe that the latter is true, he should ask the users to restate their objectives so that he can get a clearer idea of the business purpose for going ahead with the project.

This is usually a delicate matter because the executive in charge of the information systems function is generally not as conversant with the needs of the functional people as they are. Nevertheless, he must examine each request, assess it from a business standpoint, and challenge it if he does not feel that it is economically useful.

Once the needs have been determined, it is the responsibility of the information systems staff to resolve the design with the participation of the functional area. The first step is the general systems design, during and after which the executive in charge of the function must be involved to a certain extent. I don't mean, of course, that he must do the design; however, he must insure that the five basic characteristics of a successful information system—relevance, timeliness, economy, accuracy, and flexibility—will be the result. If any of those elements is missing, the chance of that system being cost effective is minimal. The executive must insure that the general systems design includes all five elements of successful systems. If he does not do that, no amount of project control from that point forth will be effective. Also, although the executive will not personally perform the design, he is completely accountable for any results, good or bad. Good tactical control without good strategic planning will help the budget somewhat but will not render an ill-conceived system cost effective.

This problem becomes somewhat more complex when a procedure exists for charging users for systems development and operational costs. This issue will be discussed in more detail later; at this point it should be emphasized that the executive in charge of the information systems function is no less responsible for examining the cost effectiveness of a proposed system if the user is picking up the budget for it. The executive will not be effective if his own information systems budget zero balances by charging all developmental and operational expenses to users but at the same time develops and operates systems which are not relevant, timely, economical, accurate, or flexible.

Information Systems Council

It is critical that there be available within the firm a group of functional representatives who can identify requirements, assess priorities, and approve any major decisions that need to be made. This Information Systems Council or Committee should be composed of people who have authority to speak for their respective functions, rather than simply of delegates who need to bring the committee's ideas back to their function for approval and review. In other words, they have to operate more like the U.S. Senate than like the United Nations.

In theory, the person selected to serve on the committee should be the head of the function, such as the vice-president of manufacturing or the vice-president of marketing. However, the drawback of that approach is that such an executive may not be thoroughly familiar with the nitty-gritty administrative problems at the lower levels of his own organization and therefore may not react knowledgeably enough to some of the operational problems that are reviewed at committee meetings. If that is the case, the executive should designate someone who is well versed in the details of the operational problems and who also has the authority to speak for the function.

However, although committee members have the authority to speak for their areas, the committee should be viewed more as an advisory body than as a decision-making body. It is unrealistic to expect this group to be able to reach the ideal of consensus about the overall priority list. Not everyone will agree with the priorities established, but each functional area must be represented on the committee; in that way, if they cannot live with the priorities established because of a planning or operational problem for which they need the assistance of information systems, they can at that time escalate their requirement to the point where it comes to the attention of each member and of the executive who serves as committee chairman. This may result in a change of priorities, but even if it doesn't the requirement will have been discussed and a business decision made not to change the priorities.

One alternative to the selection of the committee chairman would be to appoint the executive in charge of the information systems function, whether he is the controller, vice-president of finance, or president of the firm, because it is he who has the ultimate responsibility to determine which projects will be worked on and in what priority.

Another critical function of the committee is to identify the difference between the true requirements within each member's specific functional area and other requests whose validity may be in question. For example, when information systems personnel work with functional people at the operational level, the latter usually generate a wide variety of requests. Some of these are extremely valid, and others are less valid or less significant from a priority standpoint. It is sometimes difficult for the information systems person to perceive the priorities; it is also inappropriate for him to set priorities even if he is qualified to do so by virtue of an in-depth knowledge of the functional area. Furthermore, he could be working with several people in a given functional area, each of whom has his own ideas as to what should be done to serve the function. It is absolutely essential that the information systems committee member who represents that function sort out all the requests and establish one priority list for his function that is recognized as its official priority list. Without that single focus to identify functional requests, the relationship between the information systems staff and the functional personnel becomes highly subjective, emotional, and nonproductive.

It is impossible for information systems to be all things to all people, and yet many times operations are based on that belief, resulting in an ineffective information systems function with no planned program. A plan must exist. Conducting all activities on a first-come, first-served basis is all right in an automobile repair shop; an information systems function must have an overall development plan. This is not to say that emergency requests cannot be fulfilled to a certain extent. The capability to do so should exist; however, the number of emergency situations is inversely proportional to the effectiveness of the planning process.

The frequency of committee meetings depends to a certain extent on the state of the information systems function in the firm, but generally the committee should not need to meet more than two or three times a year. However, working relationships must be established between information systems people and committee members so that requirements which are identified in the interim can be placed in the proper perspective.

Identification of Requirements

This is the most difficult and yet one of the most important determinants of the cost effectiveness of the information systems function. Also, it is one matter to determine the requirements of individual areas and quite another to combine those requirements into a common list.

In many cases asking the question, What is a user requirement? is like asking, What is truth? Requirements, like beauty, are in the eye of the beholder. In other words, trying to identify requirements depends on whom you ask. For this reason, it is critical that the Information Systems Council include an authorized representative of each functional area in the firm. Once new areas of development are identified, the user should always be asked this question: How will this area aid you in running your business more effectively, and which of your objectives will this area assist in fulfilling?

Another essential point to establish is that, in the process of identifying requirements, the information systems staff not confine itself to the representative on the committee. The staff should be free to contact anyone in the firm to determine system requirements. However, it is critical that any proposed change be reviewed before implementation for viability and priority with the appropriate representative on the committee.

Personnel, marketing, manufacturing, finance, and just about every other area of the firm want information on employees, customers, products, and financial matters. The information systems staff must assess the request of each area to determine their commonality and then must take maximum advantage of that commonality in designing systems. For example, if you already have data in your files for one application, you would not request the same data from users in order to generate other output reports based on that information. And yet that very situation has happened often. People in information systems must assess each request as businessmen rather than as technicians, and must determine what information is already on file for another use before asking a user to collect it.

The information systems staff must also review the commonality of requests for future applications and combine them in order to produce a truly cost-effective function. This can only be done when the information systems people really understand the business they are serving, what the activities of the managers are, what functions the managers are controlling and operating upon, and the interrelationships of each manager's operations and decisions with the other elements of the firm. It is only when information systems people operate as businessmen that truly cost-effective systems can be produced.

Priority Setting

Priority setting is an iterative and ever-changing process for two primary reasons. First, the world of the user is constantly changing; many things that were important to him two months ago may not be as important to him as would a new problem which has arisen in the interim and which causes him to change his sense of priorities. That truism must be recognized, even though it may not be accepted with grace by many information systems staffs. Failure to acknowledge it has caused innumerable problems between functional people and information systems staffs. Ironically, the information systems people, who are generally considered the instruments of change, are the people who often do not recognize the need to change once projects have begun or even been identified.

Second, a user requirement is further defined as a systems development activity by the information systems staff during the phase of general or even detailed system design. As more is learned about the complexities of the system, and new problems are uncovered, it is not unusual for development costs to increase. This concept is well recognized in product development, where it is generally understood that the development of a new product includes a certain degree of uncertainty, and where budgets are established on the basis of what is known at a given point in time, although it is recognized that problems may arise in the development of the planned product.

However, management has not fully accepted the same logic in the area of information systems project development. It is assumed that everything is known about a project on day one, and because of that assumption budgets have been exceeded, heads have rolled, and there has been much gnashing of teeth. Not only will estimates of development costs vary as a project proceeds, but estimated operational costs will change either upward or downward, usually upward. These changes in cost estimates must be reviewed as soon as they are perceived and priorities established on the basis of this new information. However, at certain points all parties concerned must commit themselves to hard cost estimates and target dates—and adhere to them unless there is a good reason for a change.

A project high on the priority list may be much more expensive to complete than originally planned. If that is the case, management must make one of four positive decisions: (1) stop development of that project permanently, (2) place the project lower on the priority list because of its increased costs, (3) change the scope of the project so that it can be developed within the original cost estimates but somewhat reduced in scope, or (4) continue with the project at its present priority level and scope while recognizing the increased costs. The fourth alternative should be made as a positive business decision, rather than being something that sort of happens. A management control system in information systems that fails to identify those increased costs at an early stage will be disastrous and will generate unpleasant surprises that will reach the highest levels of the firm. This is poor management and should never be allowed to occur.

Strange as it may seem, some executives are unwilling to face the unpleasant responsibility of deciding not to continue a project. I have seen projects which far exceeded budget but were continued because the decision-making people, although well aware of the costs being incurred, made no positive, hard decision to stop that course of action. These situations resulted in a lessening of the initiatives of management and a continuation of the project on the basis of the general rule that a moving project keeps moving, right or wrong, unless a positive management step is taken to do something about it.

Cost Justification

This area is not generally given the attention it deserves, although everyone recognizes the need for justifying any new application effort. Too often a cost study is not undertaken to determine the complete costs both before and after development, and far too many applications are developed without that critical step. As a result, both the functional area and the information systems group are rightfully exposed to the charge that they are proceeding on an uneconomical basis.

The information systems people must supply the functional area with the costs of the system's development and operation. Of course, this is difficult to do unless the functional people clearly define what they expect from the system, how frequently reports should be run, and other basic information that goes into making up the costs of developing and operating a system. It is critical, therefore, that the specifications of the system be clearly defined and documented before the information systems staff gives hard cost estimates. While those specifications are being developed, everyone involved must recognize the fact that the effort is proceeding with a high degree of risk. General estimates can be given prior to this point; however, until the specifications of the system are defined, any cost calculations that purport to be more than ball-park estimates should be examined closely and challenged if necessary.

After the costs have been collected, the functional area is responsible for assessing the prospective application from a cost standpoint and for determining whether it is cost effective. If the system is clearly cost justified on purely tangible grounds, the decision is easier to make. If, however, the cost evaluation reveals that the system generates no savings but costs net additional dollars, the functional area must decide whether the intangible benefits make up for the difference. This is a nonquantitative analysis and therefore must be prepared to be defended on a subjective basis. If, at this point, it is determined that the system is not economically useful on the basis of either tangible or intangible criteria, it should either be eliminated or resized so that it will become an economically justifiable package.

The executive in charge of the information systems function must also pass upon the economic justification of the system. If he believes it is not justified, he must challenge the user until a meeting of minds is reached.

At this point, the question is often raised as to whether the functional area has the right to go to an outside software house to have the application developed if the executive in charge of the information systems function deems the development uneconomical. The policy on this point should be as follows: A separate decision must be made each time this question is raised. To rule out the possibility of going outside for the development of an application would be unfair to the functional area and could generate an inefficient information systems staff, because it would give them a monopoly with respect to the users. On the other hand, giving users a blanket endorsement to go outside to develop all applications would almost surely be uneconomical, because the resulting uncoordinated applications would lead to redundancies in the files, and there would be a loss of expertise by the internal information systems staff.

User Charging as a Management Tool

User charging is an excellent method of increasing the likelihood that users have economically justified their requests for information systems support. However, a user-charging system alone is absolutely no guarantee that the information systems function will be cost effective. The executive in charge of that function may believe he has been successful because all the functions for which services are performed have absorbed the entire budget. He must, however, continue to challenge each request, since it is not uncommon for a user to be willing to pick up the budget for a development effort even though it may not be economical to proceed with that effort. Allowing users free rein in this area will most certainly result in the development of some cost-ineffective systems. Two areas must be considered here: the charging out of operational costs and the charging out of systems development costs.

Operational costs. In general, it is good policy to charge out operational costs to users. When there are many users of one system, for example, when many branch sales offices use a centralized order processing system, costs should be allocated in proportion to use and measured by some equitable yardstick, such as the number of transactions entered by each location.

System development costs. For two reasons, it is not as clear whether these costs should or should not be charged out to users. First, the budgeting cycle generally takes place well before anyone can know exactly what the costs of any system development effort might be; therefore, a user may budget an unrealistic amount for the development of an unspecified system. Secondly, project cost estimates may increase as the detail system design proceeds because of the emergence of technical problems that were not anticipated at the outset. When this happens, it often makes better business sense to re-evaluate the entire overall system development plan and eliminate some other projects, possibly for other users, rather than to force the user for whom the system is being developed to increase his own budget for the newly recognized problem.

In general, then, the charging of development expenses to users tends to put a greater cost control responsibility on user management, whereas not charging development expenses to users places a greater cost control responsibility with information systems management.

Charging will tend to cause users to be more selective of projects because of the direct financial impact on their budgets.

The use of the management tool of user charging must be made on a firm-by-firm basis, considering the organizations and the people involved.

Review of Existing Systems

As part of the approach to cost-effective environmental management, the executive in charge of the information systems function should initiate and monitor a periodic review of every system that is currently in operation. A new system should be reviewed within three to six months after implementation to insure that design criteria are being met and that cost figures are not exceeding the plan either in the information systems operations budget or in the user's budget.

Once the initial review has been completed and any necessary adjustments have been made, the system should be reviewed annually. There are two reasons for this annual review: (1) to insure that the cost estimates are still valid and that no creeping inefficiency is being built into the system, and (2) to insure that the system is still relevant to the design objectives for which it was developed. In a changing environment, even a well-designed system can quickly become cost ineffective if it is not periodically reviewed for relevance.

This review can be conducted by the internal audit staff or by a joint effort of the information systems people and user personnel. Another alternative would be to use outside consultants to perform this study, which will generally result in a greater degree of objectivity. A key consideration to recognize during the review process is that continuity exists between the currently operating systems and those that are in the planning or development stages. Although it is fairly obvious that these plans should tie together, they sometimes do not do so in a medium- to large-size organization where many groups are involved in developing various systems. Redundancies will arise unless the communication between and among the groups is open and frequent.

Some information systems groups are organized so that the current systems staff forms a separate maintenance group from the systems development personnel. This organization can work out well only if the communication between the groups is effective. Without it, new systems can easily be developed with little regard for the content of existing files. Although this poor planning may result in an outstanding project control system, it will also result in a seriously cost-ineffective information systems function. Therefore, the strategy applied in the overall system development plan must complement an effective project control system in order for the function to be effective.

Confirming Major Decisions

The Information Systems Committee should be closely involved in any major decisions made by the information systems group. In addition to project identification, priority setting, and cost justification, the committee should be involved in decisions that affect selection of staff and equipment.

Staffing. Once the projects have been identified and their priorities established, the rate at which they will be developed is, to some extent, a function of the size of the development staff. This point should be presented to the committee, not necessarily for their decision or even consensus, but to give the decision maker some sense of the speed at which applications are to be developed and, therefore, a sense of the appropriate size of the staff needed.

Equipment. Major changes in equipment should also be reviewed by the committee. In most cases, its members are not technically qualified enough to judge all the details of the proposed change; however, it is important that those changes be justified economically, and that the committee generally understand well the economics of any major equipment changes.

Another consideration in making such changes is an on-line system, in which terminals would be placed in user locations. The committee should be aware of those plans and should have the right to comment on them before they become firm. It is better to discuss all the ramifications of a major change at a committee meeting than it is to face the possibility of a new perspective during the system development or implementation stage. Committee members can usually lend a functional perspective to a major change that had not been considered by the operational people, who are more closely involved in the detailed planning.

Consistency with Long-Range Planning

In order for the information systems function to be cost effective, close coordination must exist between the system development plan of the information systems group and the strategic plan for long-term growth of the firm. There are a number of ways to effect this coordination.

First, the staff person in charge of coordinating the long-range plan with the line executives should be a member of the Information Systems Committee. Second, the director of information systems should have a dotted-line responsibility for participation in the long-range planning effort. Third, both functions could be placed under the control of one executive. One possible trend in the future could be to organize the functions of finance, administration, information systems, and long-range planning under the control of one executive, who might be called the vice-president of plans and controls. This organization could tend toward a better coordination between day-to-day operations and long-range planning.

Another important goal of close coordination with the long-range planning function is to help reduce the number of crises in the information systems groups when a policy change is made which must be reflected in one or more of the operating systems. It is not unusual for the information systems group to become aware of the change only after it has been made; at that point, the group faces the crisis of changing the program to accommodate that policy change immediately, thus incurring excessive costs. Advance warning is not always possible; for example, there are times when policy changes must be made quickly to react to competitive or other pressures. However, the great majority of crises are generated by changes that were defined well before they became effective. Better communication between the planning and information systems functions would enable those changes to be incorporated within existing systems in a more orderly and cost-effective way.

Defining Working Relationships

Once a plan for systems development has been established, the proper working relationships must be established at the operational level between the systems analysts and programmers in the information systems area and people at the operational level in the functional area. Continuing dialog is needed in order to define in detail the specific methods to be employed in handling each characteristic of the system. Some decisions in this area, such as the use of either flow charts or decision tables in the program documentation, are purely technical and need not involve the functional people. Other decisions are the responsibility of the functional area and need not involve the information systems people.

However, some decisions that must be made will have ramifications that will involve both the information systems people and the eventual users. If these decisions are to be made properly, the working relationships must be established so that the information systems people have a business orientation as well as a technical orientation toward the system they are designing. Equally important, the functional people must recognize the technical problems that are involved so that they will understand the cost ramifications of the various alternatives.

Unless those working relationships are established properly, the eventual users may be forced to live with difficult or even untenable continuing operational conditions, or the information systems people may have to tolerate a user decision which could adversely affect the performance or operational costs of the system. If either of these conditions arises, the opportunity for a cost-effective system will be significantly reduced.

3

Cost-Effective
People Management

SELECTION of staff is a key aspect of cost-effective information systems. People selection, like project selection, can make or break the function. Many problems could be prevented if more careful attention were paid to selection of staff. The time invested in an extra interview, administration of an aptitude test, or detailed reference check will pay for itself many times over.

The Interview

During the interview, a specific statement of what is expected of any candidate should be spelled out in order to minimize misunderstandings and surprises after he is hired. Moreover, it is just as essential during the interview to appraise the candidate's attitude as it is to review his technical ability and applications experience. Without a positive, constructive, businesslike attitude, the most technically proficient candidate for employment will be a liability to the organization and will generate a host of id-satisfying subroutines which are not only unnecessary and difficult to maintain, but represent some of the worst kinds of cost ineffectiveness. If such a job applicant is hired, an inordinate amount of management attention will be required to correct his poor attitude and performance.

One of the best ways to motivate your staff members is to be sure that your development plan for them ties in with their future aspirations. If there is no opportunity in the firm for a good job applicant to achieve his goals no matter how outstanding his performance, that fact should be clearly spelled out to him before he is hired. If it is not, he will be a discontented employee who rightfully believes that he is entitled to a position he is not getting, and you may lose him to another company. If he does stay, he will certainly not be motivated to continue doing an outstanding job.

On the other hand, even though a staff member may be able to achieve his goal with good performance, it is bad management policy to promise him that he will achieve a given goal *on a given timetable*. It is not always within the manager's power to make such a commitment, because the final decision may be made at a higher level; furthermore, if for any reason the manager moves on to other areas, his successor will inherit the commitment, which he might judge inappropriate to fulfill. This situation would result in some serious inconsistencies between the manager and his staff. No such inconsistency should exist; therefore, don't make commitments when there is any possibility that they could not be fulfilled whether or not you as a manager are there. Turnover of good staff people is one of the most expensive kinds of cost ineffectiveness.

Consistency

It is critical to employ the same management skills in information systems that are employed in any other function.

For example, the quality of consistency cannot be overemphasized. No management position should be used for politics, game playing, or any other action that would result in losing the confidence of your people. No credibility gap should exist between what you say and what you do. The leader of the information systems function must represent the users to his own staff, and his own staff to the users, in a consistent way.

Clear Definition of Assignments

Each staff member must participate in and agree with the setting of target dates, so that when schedules are established each will be motivated to do everything he possibly can to meet or improve upon those dates.

Staff members must clearly understand the importance of the projects they are working on. If the projects are not useful or important, they shouldn't be done. It is very difficult to motivate an employee unless he knows clearly that what he is doing is useful to the firm which is paying his salary. If he doesn't understand the project, he will be poorly motivated either to complete it ahead of schedule or to look for better ways to complete it. Many information systems projects could have been much better if the people working on them had fully understood what business problem they were solving.

One of the best ways to motivate an employee is to make sure that he clearly understands the dependencies of other people or groups on his performance. The systems analyst or programmer who fully realizes the effects of his successes and failures on the organization, both within information systems and within the user's organization, will more likely be motivated to superior performance.

Performance Measurement

Performance measurement is a key aspect of people management. People need to know whether they are doing a good job and in what areas they can improve. Although it's good to set up a formal time to review these points, the manager should not wait for that time if he notices a problem that he should review immediately with the staff member involved.

Functional Orientation

The staff member must consider himself a businessman as well as a technician and strive to complete his assignment as quickly as possible rather than simply to meet his target date. The manager must be tough in working with his staff on setting target dates, but he must be equally fair when unexpected problems arise in the performance of those planned activities.

Staff members should be discouraged from discussing application problems with users in highly technical language. The use of technical jargon is usually unnecessary and tends to establish barriers in relationships with nontechnical people. There is no doubt that the use of such terminology is an irresistible temptation for some technical personnel, particularly those who do not really understand the business problem they are in the process of solving. As a rule, the amount of technical jargon used is inversely proportional to the speaker's understanding of the real problem and should be strongly discouraged. Discussions with users should deal with the business problem being solved and the more of an understanding the information systems person has of that problem, the more effective his performance will be.

4

Cost-Effective
Project Management

To be successful, a project management system must contain the same five primary characteristics as any other system—relevance, timeliness, economy, accuracy, and flexibility. The techniques employed in project control systems vary with project size, since the management requirements of a large project are different from those of a small project in many ways. A large project is defined here as one which costs more than $100,000 to develop. A medium-size project costs $30,000 to $100,000 to develop, and a small project is one which can be developed for less than $30,000.

Control Systems for Large Projects

A project control system for a large project must be highly structured and formalized. There are two basic problems in managing large projects. First, it is impossible to define in advance all the activities which need to be completed in order to complete the project successfully. This is true no matter how thorough the general system design has been by both the user and the information system staff. It simply is not possible to imagine every contingency that can occur during the detailed systems design and programming stages.

Secondly, a project control system for a large project must be formalized so that as changes occur in the project's scope or time schedules, everyone involved can quickly become aware of the effect of those changes on his own efforts. In very large projects it is impossible to call a general meeting whenever a new fact is learned, or meetings would be held all the time. However, any change should be reflected in the well-documented, explicit project control system so that each manager, systems analyst, programmer, and affected user becomes aware of it and can adjust his own priority and work schedule accordingly.

A control system for a large project should be structured in modular form. Modularity is simply a planning device which enables a large project to be broken down into a series of smaller projects so that each is of manageable size and as independent as possible from the others. Using this modular approach, as many phases can be in progress at one time as there are people to staff them. This technique allows for the greatest possible number of events to occur simultaneously, and also gives management more flexibility in assigning personnel as the various project segments are either completed or extended in scope. This increased flexibility in manpower scheduling also offers a greater opportunity for earlier completion of the overall project than would a nonmodular or a sequentially modular approach.

Nonmodular large project development efforts run into trouble because, as the inevitable unforeseen problems arise, the personnel involved find it extremely difficult to grasp the effect of those problems on the overall project, and the result is a great deal of confusion and lost time. In this situation, people tend to build in the greatest possible amount of contingency into the planning process, thus defeating the purpose of that process. As a project becomes more structured, the amount of contingency that needs to be built in is minimized, reducing cost and time estimates and improving the potential of establishing more specific controls.

In a sequentially modular approach, the project is broken down into modules. However, no two modules are in the process of being developed at the same time. In theory, this approach is the safest; in practice, it is not as practical as it appears on paper. It allows minimum flexibility in the use of manpower, will maximize the overall completion date of the project, and will often require reworking some of the modules that have been completed because of the new facts that are learned during the development of subsequent modules. This latter problem could drastically increase the cost of the project.

Any large project, no matter how it's structured, proceeds with a certain degree of risk. In order to minimize that risk, communication must be wide open. In that way, any problems will surface and can be resolved with minimal wasted effort. Periodic review sessions should be held jointly by information systems and user personnel even if no apparent problems have developed. Those meetings can be as infrequent as monthly during the early stages of development but may even be as frequent as daily during the implementation process.

Control Systems for Small Projects

In small projects, less coordination is needed and fewer unknown factors will generally arise. Therefore, the management of a small project can be less formal than that of a large project.

However, to become complacent in the management of small projects, and to assume that target dates will be met simply because the project is small, are traps into which management can easily fall. Channels of communication must be open so that problems can be recognized when they occur. If problems arise frequently, a much more rigid control system must be adopted to determine what those problems are and how to correct them so that they do not recur.

Major Project Activities

The following discussion offers some general guidelines for each major step of the development process. These steps are:

- Definition of requirements
- General system design
- Detail system design
- Programming and testing
- System test
- Implementation
- Evaluation of operational systems

On paper, this looks like a series of neat, orderly steps, each of which can be completed and evaluated before beginning the next step. However, it is never that simple. New facts will be learned as each new phase is entered, causing a potential recycling through any or all of the prior ones. To a certain extent, the amount of recycling is a direct result of the completeness of the planning of a previous phase. However, sometimes a recycling will be required even though the prior phases were thoroughly planned.

The detail system design and programming phases will overlap because it is generally not practical from a scheduling standpoint to wait until all the detailed design specifications are completed before beginning the first program. New facts learned during the programming or system test phases may cause a recycling back to the general or detailed system design phases, and may even cause a recycling back to the initial phase, resulting in a redefinition of requirements.

The two stages in which there must be little or no overlap or recycling are system test and implementation. In other words, for all practical purposes, the system must be operational at the end of system test. That phase, which will include a parallel or pilot operation, is the last opportunity to use the system in a closely controlled environment. Failure to allow enough time to thoroughly shake down the system before implementation is the greatest cause of the horror stories heard about computers. File updating programs that don't update correctly, calculations that don't work accurately, printing programs that don't print well, system controls that don't balance completely, and backup procedures that don't restore the prior condition completely are all conditions that must be resolved during the system test process. Not only must each transaction be attempted, but as many possible combinations of transactions that can be tested should be during the system test process.

It's true that a thorough, well-defined system test plan can be time-consuming and costly, particularly at a time when everyone is anxious for the system to be operational. However, failure to complete this critical step thoroughly can cause enormous hardships. It is cases such as these which give computers a bad reputation among the general public, but it is not the computer that has failed in most cases; it is management which is to blame for not allowing enough time or not thoroughly planning the system test effort.

Definition of requirements. This phase must include a clear, documented description of the business objectives of the proposed system. Whether the original idea emanates from the functional area or from the information systems group does not matter. However, both areas should participate in documenting the system objectives.

General system design. This phase is a joint effort of the information systems people and the functional people, and should produce the general flow of the system; the definition and format of all output reports; the system controls; a tentative work schedule both for the information systems people and the involved functional personnel based on estimates of systems, programming, and support time; and a general estimate of total development costs. The operational costs must also be estimated, including any savings attributable to the system. Moreover, it is critical during the general system design stage to state clearly the limit of the system's capabilities and to outline which capabilities are within its scope and which are not. A clear statement of these inclusions and exclusions will form a well-documented base point which will minimize misunderstandings as the development effort proceeds.

Detail system design. During this phase, the flow of the system must be broken down into individual tasks or programs, and a book of documentation initiated for each program. Each book must contain (1) a description and statement of purpose of the run, (2) a block diagram of its logic, (3) the record layout of all input and output files involved in the run, (4) the format of all printed forms as output of the run, (5) a clear control procedure to insure the validity of the run, (6) a clear statement of the sources of the input and how it should manually be prepared prior to processing, both by the functional people and by any input/output clerks in the computer area, (7) a plan for balancing and distributing all output, and (8) a backup plan so that the program can be rerun if problems arise during processing. Each book must also include an estimate of the time needed by the systems analyst to complete each portion of the detail system design step, plus a preliminary estimate of the programming time that will be required. Dependencies should be spelled out so schedules laid out for all the programs can be realistically combined into an overall development plan for the system.

A well-defined plan for implementation needs to be made during the detail system design phase. Included in this plan must be adequate time for a full system test, plus any parallel or pilot operation which will take place. The plan for the full-scale implementation of the live operation must be defined so that all supporting user education or reference materials required for the new system can be planned for and completed well in advance.

Programming and testing. During this phase there is great danger of time and cost overruns on the project. Most programmers have a highly technical orientation and little interest in the business goals of the project. Therefore, management of the programming effort must insure that each program is written in modular form so that it can later be maintained with a reasonable amount of effort, and that each program is well documented so that its logic is spelled out accurately on a block diagram. It is also essential to insure that the program is as simple as it can be, and that no unnecessary complexities are added to it by the programmer.

The program documentation book established during the detail system design phase should be supplemented with a record of the status of testing, plus a copy of the latest program listing.

Plans for program testing should include individual tests of each program, followed by tests of a combination of programs which make up a logical sequence of computer runs, and then by the full system test.

System test. Having previously described the significance of the system test activity, I will not review it again at this point except to state that the major reason for a failure in the system, assuming that it has been well defined, is the lack of time and attention devoted to the system test phase.

Implementation. It is critical during this phase that all activities be defined and properly staffed, both by the information systems people and by the users of the new system. User documentation and education must be planned in advance so that they can be properly executed during implementation. A reporting system must be established so that both information systems and functional management are kept up to date on the progress of the implementation program. Users must understand both the advantages and the limitations of the new system so that they will have no misconceptions about its capabilities. If the system changes the functions performed by clerical personnel, those new functions must be clearly outlined. Many clerks find it unsettling enough to have to make the transition from one routine to another; they find it doubly so if that new routine is not clearly documented or explained.

Much of the negativism that occurs during the implementation phase is not caused by a poor system but by users' lack of understanding of how to work with it. Much unnecessary pain is endured during the implementation of well-designed systems because of the absence of a well-planned implementation program.

Evaluation of operational systems. This should take place within three to six months after implementation and should measure the performance of the system in meeting the objectives set forth during the original definition of requirements phase. It should also measure the actual cost of development compared to the planned costs. The comparison of development costs is made mainly for historical purposes and for the measurement of those managing the project. The review of the system's ability to meet its original design objectives and the review of the operational costs are more actionable items.

If the design objectives are not being met, or if operational costs significantly exceed original estimates, hard decisions must be made either to continue with the system as it is currently operating, to change the system so that it will meet the original design objectives, to modify it so that operational costs are brought in line with the original plan, or to discontinue the system altogether. The latter alternative is a painful decision to make, but it must be made if, from a business standpoint, serious deficiencies or operational cost overruns exist in the system which are either uncorrectable or inordinately expensive to correct.

Project Control

Although the methods employed in setting up project control systems vary widely, the specific method used will not necessarily be a decisive factor in the success or failure of the project. I have seen complete program evaluation and review (PERT) systems in operation that weren't worth the paper they were written on only because the people who prepared the input didn't really understand the system and the managers responsible for managing the project didn't really understand the reports generated by the system and therefore could not discern any problems that arose during its operation. Since the managers didn't really use the reports, the input to the system became lax and in a short period of time failed to reflect the correct project situation. As a result, managers began using an informal yellow-pad system that really gave them the information they needed to control the project. That informal system was a much better one because of the lack of understanding of how to submit input to the PERT system and review the resultant outputs, and a lot of grief could have been averted had that been the system used initially.

It is important to estimate the specific timing of as many of the known activities as possible, and to give more general estimates of timing on the project activities that have not yet been concisely defined so that a commitment on costs is made as early as possible, resulting in changes only when there is good reason for change. If, for example, during the general system design phase an attempt is made to estimate the time for programming and testing, that estimate would have to be expressed in general terms, since at that stage the system has not yet been segmented into a defined set of programs. A better estimate can be given, however, for the time that will be involved in the detail system design phase, which will establish the needed set of programs.

It is really only the phase beyond the one in which you are currently working for which other than general time and cost estimates can be given. All activities in the next phase must be explicitly identified; management must assign clear-cut responsibilities to people for the completion of each activity; and the target dates must be established only after reviewing the assignments with those people. Management must recognize the fact that target dates can be missed, and that missing them now and then should not result in severe disciplinary action. If that were not true, time estimates given for each segment would have to include an inordinate amount of contingency in order to make absolutely sure that the target date is met.

The attitude toward the establishment and management of target dates for systems and programming time can have a dramatic effect on the cost effectiveness of the information systems organization. I would much rather see a programmer estimate a six-week completion date for a program and complete it in eight weeks than to see him estimate twelve weeks and make his target date exactly. And yet if the programmer who has been two weeks late is told that he has made a serious error, you can be sure that his next estimate will be much more conservative.

I am not saying that continuous lateness in project completion is a healthy situation, but it might be more cost effective than an organization in which all target dates are always met. What is important is that the first-line systems or programming manager have enough of a technical orientation to be able to challenge any estimate given and resolve it with the analyst or programmer by actually getting into the lowest level of detail, if necessary. If the first-line manager is not technically qualified enough to challenge his systems analysts or programmers in their time estimates, and to resolve those estimates in detailed technical terms, he will not be an effective manager of that group, not only in the original determination of target dates but also in the review of progress. In addition, management can draw on their experience by comparing time estimates with the time needed to complete similar programs or applications.

The project control system itself can be represented on large charts or graphs, a yellow pad, a PERT or critical-path program, or any other medium that is easy to update and can be readily understood by both the information systems staff and involved users. The system must list each activity, who is responsible for it, and the targeted completion date. In measuring actual performance against the plan, the system should show percentage of completion of all events that are currently in progress. That information enables management to establish an early warning system because they can see, for example, that an event which is only 30 percent complete has used up 70 percent of the planned time. If percentage completion is not shown, managers would learn that a problem exists only after the target date was missed. If they know of the problem earlier, managers may still have options which they can employ in order to complete the assignment on time.

The responsibilities listed will be primarily those of various people on the information systems staff. However, there are certain responsibilities which the system users must perform. It is just as critical to spell out those responsibilities and target dates on the same project control plan as it is to show the activities of the information systems group. In order to complete the system successfully, all events must be shown, whether they are completed in information systems or in the user's organization.

Problem Activities

A certain number of problem activities are usually overlooked at the beginning of a project. Nevertheless, they must be performed and usually cause a certain amount of cost and time overrun on projects. These activities should be defined in advance, along with all the other activities, and responsibility for them assigned and target dates established.

Test data preparation. The responsibility for this activity must be defined in advance not only because it is time-consuming but also because failure to plan adequate time for it will become a source of friction between the information systems group and the user. The information systems people should prepare the test data during the programming and testing phase, but the user should prepare them during the system test phase. In this way, the information systems people can complete programming and testing with as little involvement from the functional area as possible, and the necessary checks and balances needed during the system test operation can be provided so that the user will be sure that all possible combinations of transactions have been tested.

Review of output reports before system implementation. This is another time-consuming process, and the same ground rule should be followed; that is, the information systems people should review the reports during the programming and testing phase, but the users should review the output reports during the system test phase. No system should ever become operational before the users have given a complete and thorough review of all the output reports during the system test phase.

Establishment of supporting clerical procedures for the new system. This area also takes time to complete and is often inadequately done, so that users of a new system are not properly prepared for its implementation. This activity should be a joint effort of the information systems staff and the users. It should be clearly defined on the list of activities as an event, and should include the names of the people assigned, the amount of time needed to complete the procedures, and the target date for completion.

User education. A program must be developed to educate user management, staff, and clerical personnel. As a rule, inadequate time is allowed for this program, and some good systems have had less than optimal results simply because the users did not fully understand how to work with the system.

Documentation. Under the pressures of getting the project tested and implemented, the requirement for documentation is usually much less complete than it ought to be. I am referring here to documentation of systems, program, operations, and users. As a ball-park figure, approximately 10 to 20 percent of the systems analyst's or programmer's time should be allowed for documentation, depending on the specific system. If the schedules do not allow for that much time, the system will probably be more costly to maintain, operate, and use than would be a system with proper documentation.

If adequate time is allocated to these five problem activities, time estimates will be more realistic and will increase the potential of producing more cost-effective systems.

Reporting on Progress

One of the most critical areas in the operation of the project control system is the choice of progress-reporting techniques employed. One extremely useful technique is a detailed time-sheet accounting of system analysts' and programmers' time. Each project activity should be identified by number, and system analysts and programmers should be required to code the number of hours spent on each activity on a daily or weekly time sheet. They should also indicate the percentage of each activity which is completed so that summarization of the time sheets will show time spent on each activity against plan, and percentage completed of each activity against plan. This technique will also usually motivate the systems analyst or programmer to make better use of his time because he knows that detailed controls and measurements are being applied. The good analyst or programmer usually welcomes such a plan because it gives him an opportunity to demonstrate his efficiency. There has to be some method of accumulating the "actual" data used in any project control system, and I believe the best method is a system of time-sheet accounting.

A more summary level of progress report is the establishment of milestones, or the measurement of completion of major activities during the development of the system. Milestones should be established so that both information systems personnel and user personnel can measure their progress against completion of these milestones.

The frequency of progress reporting depends on two major factors. The first is the stage of development of the system. During the general system design phase, progress reporting can be less frequent than during the programming or system test phases. The second factor is the level of management which will receive these progress reports. The first-line manager must be posted almost daily on the progress of his staff. Higher management need be posted only at periodic intervals, except when they should be made aware of problems as they are recognized.

Another progress-reporting technique is the periodic budget review, held both with information systems management and with user management. That review considers the progress of application development compared to the budgets established for each project. The result is a status report of each project in its relationship to completion dates and budgetary controls, and may possibly cause some changes in priority based on any revised cost estimates of projects in progress. The periodic budget review is an excellent technique to determine the status of projects in progress.

A final point about project control: It is essential that a mechanism be established to resolve any problems that arise. It is one thing to have a project control system that identifies problems; it is quite another to do something about the problem. A clearly defined decision-making mechanism must be set up at the beginning of the project with the involvement of both information systems management and user management.

5

Cost-Effective
Production Management

O NE of the most critical measures of the performance of a computer system is turnaround time, which is the
elapsed time between the submission of data by a user and receipt of output by that user. The required turnaround time
should be defined during the system design stage, and everything possible should be done to insure that it will be met.

Once the system is operational, the turnaround time can
well determine the success or failure of a system. It must be
measured against actual performance, and action must be
taken if it is not being met. If, after reviewing the earliest possible time the input can be provided, the processing time, and
the latest possible time that output is needed, the turnaround
criteria are still not met, a certain degree of redesign will be
needed in order to achieve the turnaround-time requirement.

In order to meet that turnaround time, the operations staff
might have to put in excessive overtime. This fact should be

clearly spelled out when comparing the actual operations budget to the planned operations budget, and a decision must be made whether to continue with the overtime in order to meet the turnaround-time requirement or to lengthen the turnaround time in order to reduce overtime and bring operational costs back in line with plan. If significant variances occur in either timeliness or cost, it is critical that both information systems and user management be involved in selecting alternative courses of action.

It is assumed at this point that all possible operational efficiencies have already been built into the operation. These would include (1) measurement of the efficiencies of the computer operators themselves, (2) examination of the computer runs to insure that they are sequenced for optimal speed, (3) measurement of the throughput of the application to determine whether a modification in the computer configuration could enhance that throughput, and (4) examination of the schedule for providing input to the system with a view toward possibly improving its timing.

Once a turnaround time is established that is realistic to the user and makes efficient use of the facilities in the operations function, that time should become the standard against which the processing of each cycle of that system is measured. Any variances from this standard in terms of either time or cost must be explained by the operations supervisor or manager.

Measuring Actual Computer Time

Another important area to measure is the actual computer time used to process a given program or series of programs. This measurement should be made in terms of both clock time and computer meter time. Attempts should be made to have computer meter time coincide as closely as possible with clock time. Generally, the wider the gap between clock time and meter time, the less efficient is the running of a given application. Computer running times should be logged by the operators on a sheet that shows both clock and meter time for each run. The log should also show whether the run was a production run, a test, a rerun of a program, or idle time. By tabulating these run sheets, performance can be measured against pre-established standards for running each job.

These data would also provide a basis for a charging system if users are being charged on the basis of clock or meter time. If, however, users are being charged by transaction, the measurement of clock and meter time would be used more as an internal measure of efficiency than as a tool to charge computer processing time to users.

In a multiprogramming environment, the measurement of computer use becomes much more complex; in fact, no systems have yet been devised that enable the operations manager to charge out computer costs in a multiprogramming environment in a really equitable way. Computer manufacturers have designed software to perform accounting routines which are fairly good; however, they still do not give a good measure of the use of computer time plus the associated input/output devices in order to equitably charge users with the portion of the computer system they are using.

User charging in a multiprogramming environment is one of the most difficult problems today for the manager of a medium- to large-sized installation. What he must do is establish a flat rate for the use of a part, or "region," of the computer. The flat rate established is arbitrary to a certain extent, but must be based on a rate established with the objective of recovering all operational costs, which are, in turn, based on projected use. Initially this will be a trial-and-error procedure, but with good estimates of the use of each region, a charge can be established which will enable the operations manager not only to recover all expenses of the operation but also to make the planned profit if he is in charge of a profit center.

It is important that the computer operations group establish documentation standards and then rigidly enforce them. Those standards must specify precisely the information needed in order to process an application once it is operational with little or no involvement by the systems and programming staff.

Documentation should include (1) run sheets for all programs, showing the files used for all input and output by the program; (2) any operator action that might be needed in the course of processing the run; (3) the procedure for restarting the program if any processing problems are encountered; and (4) the retention cycle of all files involved in the run so that proper library procedures can be established by the operations group. When you see a systems analyst or programmer nursing an operational system closely, you know that proper standards have not been established or enforced. That is a very expensive way to operate a system.

Detailed procedures should be provided to the input/output control section so that they have a well-defined plan for the clerical processing of all data. On input, the control section should measure the timeliness of user submission of input data against the planned time for submission of those data. Many problems related to timeliness can be traced back to the fact that data were submitted late by the user in the first place. Strict balancing and editing rules must be spelled out to the input control section and administered so that the possibility of problems arising in the validity of the data is minimized. Although these manual control procedures are critical to the success of systems, they do not generally receive the attention they deserve. Of course, the user must be closely involved in these procedures, for it will generally be he who is responsible for the initial batch totaling of input data prior to their submission to the input/output control section.

On output, it is essential that the input/output control section be given well-defined procedures for tying the output reports back to a set of predefined control totals. In addition, the output function should review the quality of the output reports and set up reruns if quality standards are not met. The details of establishing procedures in the input/output control section are too often overlooked, and otherwise well-planned systems are less successful than they could be because of the credibility gap that develops when users cannot be certain of the accuracy of the output reports.

Program Testing

One of the problems in the operation of an information systems function is establishing the proper environment for program testing. From the computer operations standpoint, it is most convenient for testing to be done at one specified time, either during the day or overnight. However, setting up such a procedure would reduce the cost effectiveness of the systems and programming group by retarding progress on the development of any new application or any maintenance for systems that are already operational. This problem has been the cause of much grief to systems and programming managers and operations managers.

Generally, when target dates are established for systems development, one key criterion in establishing programming target dates is the turnaround time for program testing. For example, if a programmer is allowed only one program test a day, his progress will be significantly slower than it would be if he were allowed three tests spaced throughout the day. Therefore, the testing environment must be established so that a proper balance exists between programmer test turnaround time and impact on turnaround time of operational systems.

In the future, the majority of testing will probably be done via remote terminals at the programmer's convenience during the day. At present, however, most testing must still be scheduled at periodic intervals and should be established with the objective of minimizing application development time, while simultaneously minimizing the turnaround time of operational systems. Policy must be established in the area of test turnaround time to resolve the conflict inherent in those two objectives.

Budget Control

Strict budgetary control of the operations area is imperative. Justification of additional staff must be closely reviewed and explained before any approvals are given. If overtime is not monitored closely, it can easily get out of hand. The operations manager and any supervisors in the operations area, whether they be keypunch, input/output control, or computer operations supervisors, should be motivated to plan their activities in terms of the costs of any overtime incurred, and one of the key responsibilities of each operations supervisor or manager must be his effort to minimize overtime costs. As a rule, productivity is not equal to overtime costs for two reasons. First, overtime is generally at a premium rate. Secondly, the people performing the overtime are usually tired at that point and are operating at less than peak efficiency.

Similar attention to cost control must apply to the area of computer equipment. This cost can equal or exceed salary costs in the computer operations area. A clear procedure for the justification of additional equipment must be in place; the manager or director of information systems should be required to approve each request, and the executive in charge of the information systems function should be required to further approve any requests involving an expense above a prestated amount, such as a rental cost of $500 or $1,000 a month.

Budget controls in the area of computer supplies must also be established, and the budget should be administered closely. The costs of tapes, disks, forms, cards, or other supplies can add up very quickly and must be controlled as carefully as salary and equipment costs.

6

Organization

THERE is no one best way to organize the information systems function in the firm, or one best way to establish the organization of the information systems function itself. However, certain guidelines can be set up on the basis of the size of the firm, the significance of its information systems function, the organization of the other functions in the firm, and the nature and geographical boundaries of the firm's activities.

Information Systems Within Firm

Since the 1950s the trend has been consistently to organize the information systems function higher and higher on the organizational chart. This trend is, of course, attributable to the increasing scope, significance, and cost of the information systems function. Over the years, the function has devoted proportionately less time to the support of the financial function and more to the support of marketing, personnel, manufac-

Figure 1. In this organization, the information systems function reports to the controller.

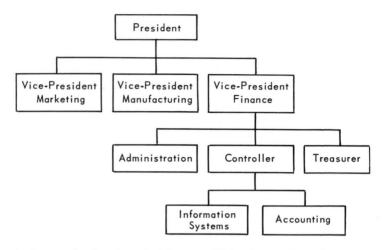

turing, and other functional areas. This change has, of course, set the stage for organizational problems, since it is less certain whether the function should continue to be organized within the financial area.

In the past, the data processing staff reported to the assistant controller. That arrangement was appropriate, since the applications performed were usually confined to payroll, billing, and one or two other activities. Today, however, it is not unusual for information systems activities to be divided more equally among all the functional areas, even to the point where the budgeted support for the financial area represents the minor portion. In this environment I do not believe that the information systems function should be organized under the controller, as it is in Figure 1.

Of course, many people believe that the information systems function is basically grounded in financial control whether it is supporting finance, marketing, manufacturing, or personnel, and that it should therefore be organized as part of the financial function. There is certainly a great deal of

60

logic to this viewpoint and, depending on the size of the firm, a reasonable solution would be to organize the information systems function under the control of the vice-president of finance, but at the same level as the controller (Figure 2), rather than to have it report to the controller. This organization gives the information systems function an opportunity to be more effective in the firm, primarily because the vice-president of finance, who would in this case be the executive in charge of the information systems function, operates at a peer level with the vice-presidents of the other functions and can, therefore, make more effective and binding decisions on the course of the information systems development effort in the firm.

For example, if the function reported to the controller it would be very difficult for him to be an effective chairman of the Information Systems Committee because he would not be operating at the same level as the other representatives on the committee. The probable result of this arrangement would be that the heads of the other functions would assign a lower-level representative to the committee rather than serving on it themselves.

In this environment, which I have seen in operation in sev-

Figure 2. The information systems function in this organization is on an equal level with the controller, and both report to the vice-president of finance.

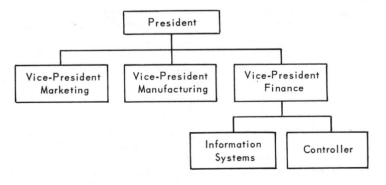

eral firms, it is difficult, if not impossible, for any clear decisions to be made on the priority of information systems development. The situation gives the director of information systems the responsibility to decide on the priority status of all the projects himself because of the lack of functional decision-making mechanism. Although it is proper for the director of information systems to compile the tentative priority list, it is not right for him to make the final decision on the development of priorities. If he does make those decisions, the executive in charge of the information systems function is abdicating his responsibilities, and the decisions will be made by the technical staff rather than by the functional staff.

Another form of organization, which is illustrated in Figure 3, requires the information systems function to report directly to the president and places it at a peer level with the vice-presidents of the other functions. Although many people in information systems advocate this organization, it should be followed only when the level of information systems activity in the firm is great enough and is an integral enough part of the overall operations of the firm to warrant the personal attention of the chief operating officer. A good example of this is the airlines industry, in which the computerized reservation system is not only an integral part of the operation of the enterprises but its very heart.

In the early 1950s, when mechanized equipment performed only the payroll preparation function for airline employees,

Figure 3. In this firm, the information systems function reports directly to the president.

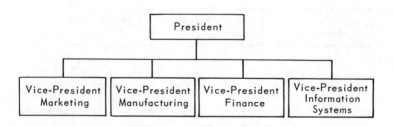

organizing the function under the controller or the assistant controller was appropriate. If it were organized that way today, the information systems function would be considerably less responsive than it needs to be to the overall requirements of the firm, from the standpoints of both day-to-day operations and future planning.

In the 1980s the large retail organizations will probably have a vice-president of information systems reporting directly to the president, because if the vision of on-line cash registers becomes a reality, information systems will be as integral a part of the retail environment as it is today in the airlines. Until that happens, however, it is sufficient in most cases for the information systems function in retail industries to be organized under the control of the vice-president of finance or even, in some cases, under the controller.

Figure 4. In this organization, the information systems function reports to the vice-president of plans and controls.

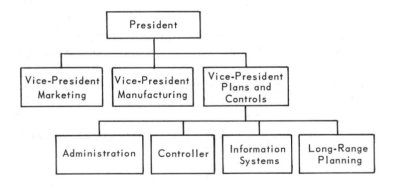

A possible organization for many firms would be to have the information systems function report to the vice-president who also has responsibility for the functions of controller/treasurer, administration, and long-range planning. He might be called the vice-president of plans and controls. Using this organization, which is shown in Figure 4, he could make sure

Figure 5. Here systems and programming are organized into two separate groups.

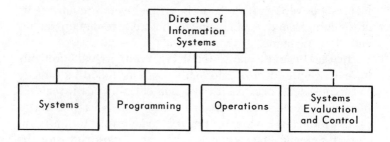

that the day-to-day operations are consistent with the long-range plans of the organization and could help to coordinate the functions of administration, controllership, and information systems, which should be closely interrelated.

Within Information Systems

There are two basic methods of organizing the systems and programming departments. The first is to organize systems and programming into two separate groups, as shown in Figure 5. The second is to combine the systems analysts and programmers into project groups, as depicted in Figure 6.

Figure 6. Systems analysts and programmers in this organization are combined into project groups.

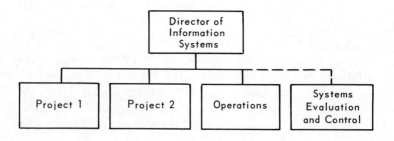

The organization shown in Figure 5 has several advantages. First, the systems group, by interfacing with all the functional areas in the firm, will be able to develop a more coordinated overall plan of systems development because all requirements will pass through that group and can be coordinated through a single focus. Secondly, the programming group will be more likely to develop a more professional breed of programmer because the programmers will be working together and will have greater opportunities to draw on each other's experience than they would if they were organized as parts of project groups.

Third, a more complete education program could be put together for the programmers than would be possible if they were within project groups. Fourth, problems in system development will be more likely to come to the surface earlier than they would if organized by project, because in a project organization the project manager will often not communicate problems upward in the hope that they will shortly be rectified. This situation has the potential of causing disastrous budget overruns unless the communication lines are unusually wide open. In the organization illustrated in Figure 5, however, the programming group will not usually accept a systems design specification unless the problem definition is very concise. Therefore, any problems in this area will probably surface earlier because of the programming group's reluctance to prepare a vaguely specified program.

The disadvantage of this organization is that the programming group is insulated from the user, and it is more difficult to instill a business orientation than a technical orientation in the programming group. Because of this, the programming group will not feel as bound by any commitments made by the systems group, and, in fact, may even take pride in lengthening the schedules which the systems group has tentatively committed to a user. This attitude will severely hamper any relationships between the information systems group and any users.

This type of organization also makes it very difficult to trace responsibility for the success or failure of a given system to the systems group or the programming group during various stages of development. The development of a system is an iterative process; it requires continued involvement by the user throughout the development process to further define the details of each transaction involved in the proposed system. The dynamics of involvement by the user, the systems group, and the programming group makes it extremely difficult in this organization either to adhere to any target dates or to assign clear-cut responsibilities. Each time I encounter an organization of this sort I have concluded that the disadvantages far outweighed the advantages.

Systems Evaluation and Control

Figures 5, 6, 7, and 8 show a function called systems evaluation and control extending from a dotted line. Whether or not this function is organized as a separate group, the functions need to be performed. This group would perform five categories of activities.

First, they would establish an education schedule for everyone in the information systems group and would do it, of course, by working with the line managers responsible for the various functions. Secondly, they would be responsible for the project measurement of planned versus actual performance and would provide the director of information systems with an internal audit so that he could review with the line managers the status and progress of each application. Third, they would establish and administer appropriate standards of documentation in the information systems group—for user, system, programming, and documentation for operations—and would also review all the documentation created by the various groups in information systems to see whether they comply with the established standards. Fourth, the group would act as staff assistant to the director of information systems on control of budgets and head count. Fifth, the systems evaluation and control group would provide technical support. Systems programmers, who are responsible for insuring that the most current level of software support is operational and also for providing guidance to the systems and programming people, would be organized in this group rather than in the operations or systems groups, thus maintaining their independence from systems, programming, and operations.

Of course, it is not absolutely necessary to organize the systems evaluation and control function as a separate group. Doing so, however, provides a series of checks and balances to insure that the functions of education, project control, standards, administration, and technical support are carried out. These functions can be conducted by the line managers responsible for systems, programming, and operations. However, I believe that a small systems evaluation and control group can greatly assist in enhancing the cost effectiveness of the information systems function.

Another organization is illustrated in Figure 7. It shows the major breakdown of the systems and programming function to be in support of the major user areas served. The illustration assumes, of course, that the major areas are marketing and fi-

Figure 7. The systems and programming function as shown here is organized to serve major user areas, and within each major area systems and programming are organized into separate groups.

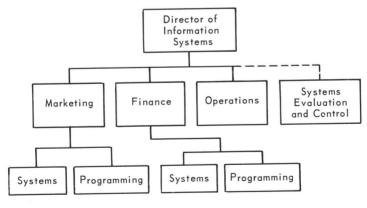

nance. There could be additional groups if, for example, there are major activities in areas such as manufacturing or personnel. This method of organization still allows for the integrity of the programming groups to remain intact as in Figure 5; however, it will lend a greater degree of user orientation to the work performed by the programming group. The coordination problems are not as great as those in Figure 5 because there is a functional focus at the second level of management coordinating the systems and programming efforts directed toward the single user. The problem under this method of organization is to make sure that the plans for the marketing people tie in with the plans for the finance people. Since they are organized separately within the information systems group, coordination would have to be the responsibility of the two second-level managers representing the marketing and finance functions within information systems and working with the director. A separate systems evaluation and control function would be effective in this case in coordinating the development plans of the different groups.

A slightly different organization is shown in Figure 8. In

Figure 8. Although the major users are represented by their information systems counterparts, the staff of each group is organized by project in this organization.

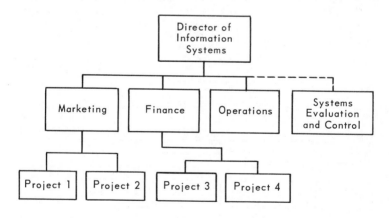

this case the major users are still represented by their information systems counterparts of marketing, finance, and any other user area. However, within each of these groups the staff is organized by project rather than separately as they are in Figure 6. This approach has the potential of generating a higher amount of user orientation within the project group because its members are motivated to produce a given project for a user. On balance, this is an excellent method of organization.

It is imperative, however, that second- and third-level management make sure that the lines of communication are wide open so that problems bubble up before they become too big to handle. In a project environment communication is one of the most difficult problems to manage, particularly if no separate systems evaluation and control group exists to review progress.

A disadvantage of this organization is that systems analysts and programmers will be transferred from one project to another as manpower requirements for each project change. To some extent this has an unsettling effect on the staff.

Assuming competent management in all four examples, I believe that the project organization represented in Figures 6 and 8 will be the most productive. One key disadvantage of the organizations depicted in Figures 5 and 7 is that they require a clear distinction to be made between a systems analyst and a programmer. That is an unrealistic distinction because the majority of development personnel can operate as programmer/analysts to varying degrees. Some people are primarily analysts, but can do some programming, and others are basically programmers and yet can do some analytical work. I believe that establishing an organization which does not recognize the existence of the programmer/analyst will reduce the flexibility within the information systems staff and will not take full advantage of each person's capabilities.

About the Author

Burton J. Cohen is director of firm information systems at Touche Ross & Co. Before taking that position he was with IBM, serving successively as systems engineer, instructor, systems engineering manager, manager of field implementation for IBM's advanced administrative system (an internal real-time system), and manager of information systems planning and development at IBM's World Trade Headquarters. Mr. Cohen, who holds a B.S. degree in accounting from Temple University, has been a frequent guest speaker at AMA seminars.